comfort
prayers

comfort prayers

Prayers and Poems to Comfort, Encourage, and Inspire

June Cotner

Andrews McMeel Publishing®

a division of Andrews McMeel Universal

Andrews McMeel Publishing
a division of Andrews McMeel Universal
1130 Walnut Street, Kansas City, Missouri 64106

www.andrewsmcmeel.com

16 17 18 19 20 SHO 10 9 8 7 6 5

ISBN: 978-1-4494-4601-7

Library of Congress Control Number: 2014932026

ATTENTION: SCHOOLS AND BUSINESSES
Andrews McMeel books are available at quantity discounts with
bulk purchase for educational, business, or sales promotional use.
For information, please e-mail the Andrews McMeel Publishing
Special Sales Department: specialsales@amuniversal.com.

For Kyle and Kirsten—
you both inspire me!

CONTENTS

∽ *seven* ∽

GRATITUDE 105

～ *eight* ～
INSPIRATION 117

THANKS

This book would not have come about without the support of a loving family; my dedicated agent, Denise Marcil; a talented and caring editor, Patty Rice; the backing of an enthusiastic publisher, Andrews McMeel Publishing; and wonderful selections received from countless contributors.

I feel especially blessed by the joys of my family: my husband, Jim Graves; my daughter, Kirsten Casey; my son, Kyle Myrvang; and many dear relatives in my extended family—who all give me comfort in their own ways.

In all, more than 4,000 submissions were considered for *Comfort Prayers*. That's on top of favorite selections I've collected for all my anthologies, culled from more than 1,000 books.

My life is so blessed by my acquaintance with over 900 regular contributing poets to my anthologies. I'm grateful for their talent and enthusiasm.

Pulling double duty critiquing the manuscript were my two employees Kirsten Casey and Robin Rebecca Carter, without whom this book not have happened.

The following individuals at Andrews McMeel Publishing have been very enthusiastic and extremely supportive in promoting my books: Patty Rice, senior editor, and Kathy Hilliard, publicity director.

In addition to being very labor intensive, creating anthologies is an expensive endeavor. I'm especially grateful to publishers and license holders who recognize this and either waive or reduce their permission fees so that all of us can benefit from the words of grace and wisdom contained in *Comfort Prayers* as well as other anthologies.

My last and most sincere thanks goes to the Divine One for allowing me to share these many messages of solace to ease and comfort our souls during difficult times.

LETTER TO READERS

Thy fate is the common fate of all,
Into each life some rain must fall.

This quotation, attributed to Henry Wadsworth Longfellow, has always given me comfort. These words and many others in this book illuminate the simple truth that no human is exempt from their own set of challenges. The message that the fate of humanity is to confront and overcome life's inevitable trials gives me a sense of the collective strength of the human spirit.

But there are times when our circumstances are more than simple "rain." When we feel more like the victims of a treacherous storm—or a hurricane or a blizzard—and are completely overwhelmed, forced to confront adversity that seems beyond our resources. Unthinkable events will occur that test the limits of human endurance. Knowing that others have gone before and survived helps ease our pain and anxiety. It's during these times that I hope this book will provide solace, comfort, and perhaps even perspective.

There have certainly been times when I have felt so overcome as to have doubted my own ability to cope, yet, have somehow found the strength to gather my courage and continue on. This strength has come from the most surprising of sources. Perhaps from a sympathetic friend, from some voice within, or even from a fortune cookie's musing I happened to have absently stashed in my wallet and then stumbled upon just at the right moment.

This collection is intended to be that friend, that inner voice, or that saved quip. The words and notions contained herein have come to me throughout my years of collecting for other volumes of poetry and prayers. Since being moved by the first comforting pieces I received, I have always known that one day I would compile a volume specifically to provide solace on dark days—to spread empathy, share the burden, and nurture the strength of the human soul.

Anyone who has pondered the mystery of human suffering has surely asked the rhetorical question, "Why?" Perhaps suffering is a hidden gift, for what purpose could our trials serve other than to find and discover comfort in one another, in our faith, and in ourselves? I strongly believe that the times of most difficult challenge are a divine method of bonding us to one another and discovering our inner resources, thereby enriching the human spirit. I hope you find the words in this book will soothe your soul while providing comfort, encouragement, and inspiration.

one

COMFORT

WHERE I'M BOUND

I am looking for comfort.
They tell me all I have to do is ask
and you will help me.
Simply.

I am in need of peace.
They urge me to turn to you
and you will grant my wish.
Silently.

I am searching for happiness.
They tell me to open my heart
and you will fill it with love.
Sweetly.

I am listening and
I promise to accept your truth.
Sincerely.

⤳ LORI EBERHARDY

RESILIENCE

Though bowed,
     You are not broken.
Though stretched,
     You're strong, my friend.
You are resilient like a willow—
You'll find your spring again.
Though your branches
     Now weigh heavy,
Your roots go deep and true.
This is just a change of season—
God has better plans for you.

〜 SHARON HUDNELL

PRECIOUS LORD, TAKE MY HAND

Precious Lord, take my hand.

Lead me on. Let me stand.

I am tired. I am weak. I am worn.

Through the storm,

Through the night,

Lead me on to the light.

Take my hand, precious Lord,

and lead me home.

∽ THOMAS A. DORSEY

A GENTLE PRESENCE

I know your spirit can hear me
so I hold your hand and tell you I am here.
I encourage you to be strong.
I pray for you every night and you are
in my thoughts every day.
You are teaching me patience and
helping me to be more faithful.
I know at times you do not feel close to God,
and your life's hardships
have left you questioning His love for you.
But God has chosen you.
He is using you to educate, to enlighten,
and to remind us not to take life for granted.
Remember that hope is what will sustain you
and faith will always set you free.

God is working miracles through you
so be still and listen.
Surrender to His power and once you let go,
the healing process will begin.

∾ LORI EBERHARDY

ALONE

When you feel you are alone
Remember there are angels
Whose sole purpose
Is to embrace the lonely

~ CORRINE DE WINTER

THE ANGEL APPEARS

Sometimes the angel appears in the form of a friend who says exactly the words we need to hear that day. Or you will unwillingly act as an angel to someone else, tossing off a message so casually that, though it saves another person's life, you hardly remember the moment at all.

— SOPHY BURNHAM

IT WAS JUST A HUG

out of nowhere
from my three-year-old.
In the softness
of his encircling arms,
and velvet cheek
pressed to my side,
I thought, please,
in times ahead
of anger, pain,
and disappointment,
when fate crushes,
love wounds,
and friends betray,

let me recall
this moment as
a blanket around
my heart.
Many years later,
I still do.

⌐ ANN REISFELD BOUTTÉ

ALL THINGS PASS

All things pass
A sunrise does not last all morning
All things pass
A cloudburst does not last all day
All things pass
Nor a sunset all night
All things pass
What always changes?

Earth . . . sky . . . thunder . . .
  mountain . . . water . . .
  wind . . . fire . . . lake . . .

These change
And if these do not last

Do man's visions last?
Do man's illusions?

Take things as they come
All things pass

◆ LAO-TZU
   (adapted by Dr. Timothy Leary)

CHANGES

Storm settles into quiet,
Darkest dusk leads to a dawn,
Bleak winter melts to springtime,
And the tide turns—
     Hold on.

❰ SHARON HUDNELL

two

FAITH

FOSTERING FAITH

Never lose sight of what once enchanted you.
As dawn turns to dusk, it is normal
for colors to fade.
But morning always follows,
Renewing each of life's miracles,
And fostering faith in a better tomorrow.

↜ HEATHER BERRY

I HAVE LOST NOTHING

I have lost nothing
in my life
that I could not find again
with God.

— CORRINE DE WINTER

TO LIFE

Dear Life, oh dearest
come with me
wherever I go,
even when I drop
this fading body, come
oh beautiful Life, and keep on
coming, flowing, streaming,
dreaming fearless, loving, wanting,
sweet Life, with your magic
dance of miracles
juggling balls of light,
your supreme womanly form

laughing down the cosmos,
your myriad jokes and jewels and truths,
your pure happy Self
that ensouls the universe,
Come, my Love, and always be
and never leave, beloved Life.

～ JANINE CANAN

DEAR GOD, PLEASE TAKE MY HAND

Dear God, please take my hand and help
   me walk through this fire.
Don't let me slip away, please hold me
   in your power.
Help me see the light and to hold on
   tight, to have faith.
Help me to learn what it is you want
   me to learn.
Help me retain my dignity and help me
   to accept what I can't change.
Guide me . . . sit in my heart.
Don't allow despair to swallow me.
Please God, show me a road out of here.
Help me find the strength to cope . . .
   and to grow.

Help me regain my health . . . please God.

Carry me if I can no longer manage to
   stand,

and set me under the shade of your tree
   so I can heal.

Please show me the path to peace, and
   mend my heart.

God, I am powerless in this valley of pain,

please lift me up and always let me know
   your presence.

Please be in my heart and take my
   shaking hand.

Amen.

꙳ SHERRY LARSEN

BELIEVE

Believe you will emerge from this healthier,
with a greater knowledge and respect
for the body you were given.
Believe your family and friends,
all the people you've touched,
and some you may not even be aware of,
are praying for you to come through this
    well and strong.
Believe in the compassion and skill
of your doctors, your nurses,
and the loving care of your angels.
Believe life holds many wonderful moments
    in store for you
and much for you to accomplish
    along the way.

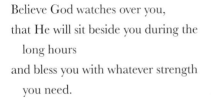

Believe God watches over you,
that He will sit beside you during the
    long hours
and bless you with whatever strength
    you need.

↬ SHARON HUDNELL

FAITH

When my friend calls, long distance,
early one Saturday morning, I listen,
knowing there's something wrong,
think it's her eighty-year-old mother,
surely not her, she's younger than I am,
only forty. When she says,
"I have breast cancer," there's a quiet
on the line, as I search for something
to say. And then she tells me it's spread
to her spine, and there are no words for this.

And because there is nothing I can do,
I go out to the garden, dig the hard March
ground, turn over ice crystals in the cold dark
soil, and plant peas, little grey pebbles, tuck
them in with a slap and a chink
that might be a substitute for prayer.

For in spite of everything, June will come
again, and those little pairs of leaves
will make their run for it, ladder up the air.
And these peas will fill their pods
with sweet green praise.

⌁ BARBARA CROOKER

I AM NOT AFRAID

I am not afraid of storms,
for I am learning how
to sail my ship.

∾ LOUISA MAY ALCOTT
   (1832–1888)

RELEASE

Tears are the tips of those sorrows
we choose to let go.
And so, as I cry out to You, Lord,
I ask You to help me release
all that has been binding my heart.
As I feel yesterday's sadness
running down today's face,
my still moist eyes begin
to look forward to tomorrow.
And with Your grace,
I feel myself remembering
how to smile once again . . .

⌐ ANNE CALODICH FONE

PERSEVERANCE

There are moments on this earth
when we experience terror
of knowing how utterly alone we are,
helpless moments when our spirit is silent,
and our cries echo hollowly in our ears.

Then we must remain steady like the mighty oak,
and supple like the graceful birch
until that blessed moment, awaited in faith,
when the sun shines, the weather clears
and the sap within starts to run again.

↶ MARYANNE HANNAN

RENEWAL

Imagine not that life is all doing.
Stillness, too, is life;
and in that stillness
the mind cluttered with busyness quiets,
the heart reaching to win rests,
and we hear the whispered truths of God.

— RABBI RAMI M. SHAPIRO

TRUST GOD

The wisest people are those who, although
unrelenting in their quest for answers,
trustingly leave some of the problems
in the hands of God who knows the whole.

～ REVEREND DALE E. TURNER
  (1917–2006)

KEEP THE FAITH!

I have come to the conclusion that the most
important element in human life is faith. From
faith, and through it, we come to a new understanding of ourselves and all the world about us.
It puts everything into a spiritual focus . . . so
that love and joy and happiness, along with
worry, sorrow, and loss, become a part of a large
picture which extends far beyond time and space.

ROSE FITZGERALD KENNEDY
(1890–1995)

THE PROMISE

Pain issues from a fractured soul,
the broken root of the tree.
Tomorrow new leaves and buds
will bubble out of the
appearance of dead branches,
not because we stop grieving,
not because we know how,
not because we are worthy,
but because that is the way of life,
the grace of pulse for every living being.

✍ MARIAN OLSON

three

COURAGE

COURAGE

Heroes do not wear courage
across their chests like banners,
large letters, screaming lion heartedness.
Instead, courage grows slowly
through the years, along with character,
burrows deep in the gut,
just waiting for the right mixture
of adrenaline and circumstance,
then like fire, igniting dynamite,
explodes into brilliant acts of valor.

◦ SUSAN ROGERS NORTON

WHAT COUNTS

What counts is not necessarily
the size of the dog in the fight—
it's the size of the fight in the dog.

⟿ DWIGHT D. EISENHOWER
   (1890–1969)

ENDURANCE

We never have more than we can bear. The present hour we are always able to endure. As in our day, so is our strength. If the trials of many years were gathered into one, they would overwhelm us . . . but all is so wisely measured to our strength that the bruised reed is never broken.

      ⌐ H. E. MANNING
        (1808–1892)

STEPPING STONE

I do not ask to walk smooth paths
nor bear an easy load.
I pray for strength and fortitude
to climb the rock-strewn road.

Give me such courage and I can scale
the headiest peaks alone,
And transform every stumbling block
into a stepping stone.

∽ GAIL BROOK BURKET

THE SAILOR

I am not free
for the I that speaks can only be my soul
and the soul is bound by the body.
Like an incarcerated sailor that has been
  lashed to the mast,
I cling to my wooden haven and ride out
  the storms and the calm.
Yet my resolve is not shaken,
for I will learn from every wave that
  pounds the bow,
and every sway from gentler seas.

I will scan the skies and gaze upon the waters
and feel the wind against my skin,
always searching for a hint of direction.
And when my ropes are finally cut,
I will have become something that I am not . . .
something better.

— JOHN S. FANUKO

LEARN TO ACCEPT WHAT IS

We can never know what strengths and revelations
might be on the other side of our fears until we
face them and feel them all the way through.
True positive thinking is the mental stance of
surrender, simply trusting the process. We learn
to accept what is.

⊸ JACQUELYN SMALL

GIVE ME COURAGE

When I feel threatened
or believe myself to be a failure,
give me courage to enter my still center,
the place of buried treasure
and sunshine
and solitude,
where you are, Lord,
and where it no longer matters
who approves of me
or how successful I am
because you are there,
and, in your presence,
I rediscover the confidence
to be me.

↝ ANGELA ASHWIN

SPLENDOR IN THE GRASS

Excerpt from "Intimations of Immortality
from Recollections of Early Childhood"

Though nothing can bring back the hour
Of splendor in the grass, of glory in the flower;
We will grieve not, rather find
Strength in what remains behind; . . .

WILLIAM WORDSWORTH
(1770–1850)

THE GRASP OF YOUR HAND

Let me not pray to be sheltered from dangers, but to be fearless in facing them.

Let me not beg for the stilling of my pain, but for the heart to conquer it.

Let me not crave in anxious fear to be saved, but hope for the patience to win my freedom.

Grant me that I may not be a coward, feeling Your mercy in my success alone; but let me find the grasp of Your hand in my failure.

↘ RABINDRANATH TAGORE
(1861–1941)

DON'T WISH ME HAPPINESS

Don't wish me happiness—I don't expect to be happy all the time, but it's gotten beyond that, somehow. Wish me courage and strength and a sense of humor—I will need them all.

∾ ANNE MORROW LINDBERGH
(1906–2001)

A DEFINING MOMENT

When a defining moment comes along, you can do one of two things. Define the moment, or let the moment define you.

~ JOHN NORVILLE AND RON SHELTON
FROM *TIN CUP*

WHAT IS MISSING

There are days when darkness
Descends over every corner
Of our world,
And all we know is what is missing.
These are the times
We are meant
To take what is still before us
And build on it, cherish it,
Bring the present into bloom again.

∾ CORRINE DE WINTER

four

HOPE

WHO WOULD HAVE HOPED

Who would have hoped
rage would turn to grief,
that grief would find comfort,
that healing balm could flow.

O faithless heart, remember this—
all you dream can wither
or bear fruit. Therefore, take courage
on those desperate nights.
Perhaps joy is on its way.

∾ SUSAN LANDON

ACCEPTANCE

It's in grief's darkest hours when
We really need to know
That only in acceptance can
New hope begin to grow.

Acceptance when it finally comes
Begins to bring relief
As healing hope renews our souls
And strengthens our belief—

Light can emerge from darkness when
Acceptance shows its face,
As we allow ourselves to heal
Through God's own love and grace.

~ HILDA LACHNEY SANDERSON

SOMETIMES I AM STARTLED
OUT OF MYSELF,

like this morning, when the wild geese
came squawking, flapping their rusty
hinges, and something about their trek
across the sky made me think about
my life, the places of brokenness,
the places of sorrow, the places
where grief has strung me out to dry.
And then the geese come calling,
the leader falling back when tired,
another taking her place. Hope
is borne on wings. Look at the trees.
They turn to gold for a brief while,
then lose it all each November.
Through the cold months, they stand,
take the worst weather has to offer.
And still, they put out shy green leaves

come April, come May. The geese glide
over the cornfields, land on the pond
with its sedges and reeds. You do not
have to be wise. Even a goose knows
how to find shelter, where the corn
still lies in the stubble and dried stalks.
All we do is pass through here,
the best way we can. They stitch up
the sky, and it is whole again.

↪ BARBARA CROOKER

COLLECTING LIGHT

Across the street
a neighbor strings white lights
along the eaves of his house.

Across the world
they sleep out in the cold,
our neighbors too,
wakened by gunfire.

I see the way the chickadees
take turns at the feeder.
I watch a woman take
her husband's hand.

I see the way the sun will find
the only interruption
in dark clouds,
to toss this amber light
across the pines.

I watch the way a young man
lifts his mother from
the wheelchair
to the car,
the shawl he lays
across her lap.

I save up every scrap
of light,
because I know that it will take
each tiny consolation
every day
to mend the world.

⌁ DEBORAH GORDON COOPER

JUST FOR TODAY

Just for today,
I will strive to recognize
The beauty within myself.
I will escape discouragement
And replace it with virtue.
I will offer compassion
And forgive my faults.
I will bury self-doubt
And plant seeds of optimism.
I will cast out bitterness
And treasure purity.
Today . . .
I will embrace every good thing
And surrender myself to God.

✍ LESLIE A. NEILSON

MAY WE NEVER GIVE UP HOPE

May we never give up hope, whatever the terrors, difficulties, and obstacles that rise up against us. May those obstacles only inspire us to even deeper determination. May we have faith in the undying love and power of all the enlightened beings that have blessed and still bless the earth with their presence. May the visions of so many mystic masters of all traditions of a future world free of cruelty and horror, where humanity can live on earth in the ultimate joy of union, be realized through all our efforts.

✦ ANDREW HARVEY

A PRAYER FOR HOPE

Dear God,

Please give me the strength to hope.

Turn my bleak thoughts

into gentle encouragement.

Let me feel hope

and believe that all is not lost.

And finally, allow that hope

to fuel my courage to carry on.

Amen.

∽ KIRSTEN CASEY

AFTER THE PINK SLIP

Monday morning,
I was a plant uprooted,
Leaves drying,
    Shriveling,
Beneath a heartless sun.
Thank You for sending me
    The deep nourishment of patience,
    The clear water of optimism,
    And the healing warmth of faith.
Soon, I will find new soil
    In which to grow and be productive.
Soon, I will put down roots
    And start again.

∽ SHARON HUDNELL

HOPE IS OUR INSTINCT

By nature we feel hope when tragedy occurs.
Hope is our instinct.
Embrace it.

✎ KIRSTEN CASEY

WORRY BALM

Good will prevail
Peace will come

Open your heart
to welcome them

〜 ARLENE GAY LEVINE

HOPE

Winter sunlight, fool's gold, pours in the
    south window,
fails to warm. Weak as tea, pale as bone,
    insubstantial
as dust on a mantle, water falling over
    stone.
The ground outside, hard, white as the
    hospital bed
where my friend waits after her marrow
    transplant,
hoping her white count will rise. I watch
    birds at the window—
sparrows, titmice, finches—the plain
    brown, the speckled,

the ordinary, no flashy travelers up from
   the tropics,
where winter is a verb, not a state of the
   heart.
I go out to fill the feeder, feel silky grain slip
through my fingers: millet, proso, corn.
   Little birds,
little angels, singing their small song of
   consolation.
A thin drizzle of sun slips through clouds,
a strand of hope against the icy odds.

✺ BARBARA CROOKER

BEGINNING AGAIN

Always there is hope:
Daylight after every night
Sunlight after rain.

∽ MICHAEL S. GLASER

five

HEALING

PLEASURES

Find pleasure in the little things—
Ice cream in a cone;
Raking October's leaves;
Spending time alone.

Tossing pebbles in a stream—
Chasing rainbow's end;
Running through the morning grass;
Talking with a friend.

Find pleasure in the little things
For little things can bless.
They brighten up a weary day
And make your worries less.

⌐ JOAN STEPHEN

GOING TO A SPECIAL PLACE

I think everyone has a place for healing, though
they do not always give it a name. As a child
I didn't know that rock was my healing-rock.
It is only now as I pray with these memories that
I realize what was happening at that rock. The
rock was the place I went when I was afraid or
confused. It was a place of healing for me. It did
more to soothe my soul than any confessional.

➴ MACRINA WIEDERKEHR

MEMO

Walk along a summer-splashed beach.

Let the ocean tickle your toes.

Sit under the arms of a friendly tree.

Sky-gaze into cotton cloud sculptures.

Gather bouquets of rainbow flowers.

Embrace their fragrance, their fragility.

Take a journey through pages of books.

Sleep under midnight stars and make wishes.

Plant a garden of friendship and nurture it.

Reap the rewards of conversation and sharing.

Let the sun warm you and renew your spirit.

Let the laughter of children melt your heart.

Rest, reflect, and rejuvenate.

Remember all the moments that were golden.

✓ JUDITH A. LINDBERG

PEACE

Let the rain wash you clean,
and let the sun dry your tears.
Allow the comfort of the angel wings
gently wrapped around you
to rock you to sleep.
The night will offer you peace,
and the morning promises to bring joy.
Believe, and there will be a sweet spirit
that will bring you home again.
Now your soul is free.

— LORI EBERHARDY

COIN OF THIS REALM

This is not despair,
not the retreat into the deep wound
but a conscious living of each day

This is the placing of one foot before
   the other,
not the free stride of the unencumbered
but the careful tread of the initiated foot

This is learning how to walk
without familiar landmarks, alone
even in the company of others,
not ready yet for new direction

This is the living of each day, aware
that what you cannot predict
may still loose sudden tears, yet
that laughter too is possible

This is when you struggle
as plants in arid soil
strive without conscious knowing
to stay alive until the rain

This is a time for faith
that this most naked agony of loss
will ease, and not corrode the spirit

This is the time to trust that day after
labored day you will move forward,
open to joy as well as pain;
two-sided coin, you proffer for remembrance

> MAUDE MEEHAN
  (1920–2007)

CELEBRATION

From the first flutter of dove gray light
with eyes still soft from sleep
mind dancing between this world and dream
begin to say, like a chant heard before birth
forgotten when waking here on earth,
"I celebrate this day"

Bless air as it rushes into lungs
expanding them and consciousness
Experience the kingdom: svelte hollow of
    lover's neck,
tangerine chill of sweet sourness,
green hills transforming to gold as seasons
give way only to return with the scent
of rain-soaked blossoms

Bless the bounty of the miraculous ordinary
and say, "I celebrate this day" even as emotions
deeper than sadness, more fierce than joy
bombard your heart with questions
never meant for answering, even as
the baby cries and bombs explode
recall the gift of another soul holding
your eyes in a knowing beyond words
and say, "I celebrate this day"

∽ ARLENE GAY LEVINE

CRY

The only way you can truly recover from tragedy is to grieve. So don't be afraid to let yourself cry. Crying does not make you weak. Cry and cry often. Let your tears become the rain that cleanses and heals. Grieve for all you have lost. Grieve because the whole world seems against you.

Once you have healed—you will look back on the time spent grieving and be thankful for the strength it gave you to eventually overcome the tragedy.

So don't be afraid to let yourself cry.

＞ KIRSTEN CASEY

PAIN AND SUFFERING

Pain and suffering may often seem to be calling us to jump in and fix things, but perhaps they are asking us first to be still enough to hear what can really help, what can truly get to the cause of this suffering, what will not only eliminate it now but prevent it from returning. So before we act, we need to listen.

꙳ MIRABAI BUSH

CUTTING OUR HAIR
BEFORE CHEMO

We watch our ears emerge timid and huge
like a newborn with sudden space to unfold
fragile, yet trusting of love.

We cut it to the hard curve of our heads,
a jagged line, silver and black, across our
   napes
bristles standing guard over the chemo drip.

We'll watch our hair grow back, together.
We, who are within an inch of our lives
will cherish each sign of health—

We'll hear the possibilities curl around us
a tangible song of healing and joy
a duet of hope celebrated one beautiful
strand at a time.

～ PAMELA BURKE

BOUND ANGLE

If you could call it perfection
what would it look like?
How would you know it,
feel it,
be it?

Wherever you are now
call it perfection
and know
that in this moment
it is really enough.

    ↝ LEZA LOWITZ

WHEN A MARRIAGE FAILS

Out of mud the bluest flower
opens in the sun
    unashamed,
        without anger or regret;
neither more or less than what it is,
alive again and free.

∽ MARIAN OLSON

LAUGHTER AND FUN

A complete revaluation takes place in your
physical and mental being when you've laughed
and had some fun.

              — CATHERINE PONDER

six
REFLECTIONS

TWILIGHT

One cannot measure a lifespan.
Calendars cannot count moments.
The sunsets of twilight, the promise of dawn
Do not truly capture forgotten youth,
Those carefree days of long ago.
Life is told by the wisdom of wrinkles,
Genuine laughter, strength of heart,
And yes, even the bittersweet memories.
Blessings shower each of us in temporary
    crowns.
When we count decades as reality,
We know that we must savor the sunsets now,
Share them with those we love,
And keep those we have lost close in our hearts
Forever.

∽ JUDITH A. LINDBERG

AFTER THE FUNERAL

And so, we ask ourselves, what now?
What, when the coffin jolts and drops,
the tiny shovel passes hand to hand,
all the mourners turn away,
relieved and sad, and half afraid,
and half convinced that flower-laden
journey down into the hot red earth
will always, only, be for someone else.

What now? we ask, and looking down, look up
at how the sky is, somehow, bluer overhead
today, the grass more lush. A bright green beetle
scuttles on the path, a catbird mews. The sun
leaps in the sky, sets orange maple leaves
insistently ablaze with life.

↝ JOANNA CATHERINE SCOTT

WHEN THE DARKNESS IS DEEP

When the darkness is deep, figures
begin to appear at the place where
you and sky collide. First they
resemble the ones you drew as a kid.
Then, like your body, they blossom,
fill the space between you and mystery.

When the deep is dark, larger figures
appear, yours and not yours, now
and much later in the place without clocks.
But now is, as when on the phone
you said, *Now I feel good.*

So when darkness takes you down
with her vast tender hands, trust in the earth
of her making, in the yeast of your fear,
the water of your courage, the heat
of your good heart. For you will rise up
over and over after being pressed lovingly
down just the right number of times
to be covered, baked in the heat of her hands
until you become the finest bread
which family, friends, neighbors,
even strangers in shops will see, taste and
ask: *What is the recipe for that?*
How can I become that?

∽ GENIE ZEIGER
  (1943–2009)

TOMATO WORMS

There are the joys of tomatoes,
luscious, red and bursting,
warm from the garden,
sensuous like late summer.

And then there is the matter
of tomato worms and crop dust,
the sweaty details
of planting and pruning,
weeding and watering.

Days are like that:
some are ripe and luscious,
basking in the heat of harvest;
others are lean and silent,
filled with the stirrings
of strange new feelings.

✎ SUSAN LANDON

CAPTAINS OF OUR OWN SOULS

The human heart carries hurts through life.
We are all scarred, burdened, and broken in
different ways. Many of these injuries are
unavoidable. We cannot escape the losses that
life brings. But we control whether our souls are
tied in knots, angry, and gnarled. We cannot
control the world, but we are each of us the
captains of our own souls.

— RABBI DAVID WOLPE

TRAVEL

I have been to the Grand Loneliness
Do not think you may
travel there uninvited
It must call your name
Do not imagine what the terrain is like
You can not
Only the gifts you return with,
richer than the million brilliant things
of this world, will hint
at what has been gained and
what has been lost on such a journey
If you have been
we can recognize each other
by the dark calm of our eyes
the drumbeat of our hearts
emptied to fullness

↝ ARLENE GAY LEVINE

SUFFERING ARRIVES WITH A GIFT

Suffering arrives with a gift.

Suffering has a purpose.

Suffering wants you to wake up.

Suffering will wait for ages.

Suffering knows what is real.

Suffering is so deep she goes all the way.

Suffering plunges into your blood.

Suffering opens your darkest closet.

Suffering waters your dusty garden with
   her tears.

Suffering holds the golden keys.

Suffering is devoted as a mother wolf.

Suffering watches you shake in fear and
   fall to your knees sobbing.

Suffering is the supreme teacher.

Suffering takes you behind the glitter.

Suffering leads you to God.

Suffering is a moody poet.

Suffering makes poetries, paintings, and symphonies of sorrow.

Suffering is a vast cathedral.

Suffering is a fast foaming river.

Suffering is an old workhorse.

Suffering is a melting sun.

Suffering dances madly with Joy.

Suffering is the wind that sweeps your heart clean.

Suffering is the messenger who rides the rainbow.

Suffering is driven to find your destiny.

Suffering hungers for your burning core.

Suffering is a tough officer of peace.

Suffering's eyes are mirrors of mystery.
Suffering washes a tiny sand dollar up on
the shore.
Suffering shines her flashlight in the dark.
Suffering is the holy wanderer who searches
for your soul.
Suffering is your sacred spouse.

Friend, don't waste her extravagant love.

⋙ JANINE CANAN

THE PUDDLE-JUMPER

She's all of four
with long blonde ringlets,
tall rubber boots,
and a shy, bright smile.

It's January.
Boston has no snow,
but there's a puddle
in the parking lot.
She wades right in,
a little duck whose feathers
are a mop of curly hair.

She's halfway to her knees,
all smiles, her Mom
and Dad enthused.
It helps to see her play.
My days of late
have been so dark.
The rays of light
so very small.

∽ SUSAN LANDON

TRUST LIFE

Trust life, and it will teach you, in joy and sorrow,
all you need to know.

⇛ JAMES BALDWIN

WINTER FIELDS

The field lies fallow
after the yield has been gathered,
dirt drifting into the hedgerows.
Sparrows eat fallen seeds
And snow sifts over the furrows.
A young fox passes this way.
At night rabbits play here
in the cold moonlight.
So a man, within himself,
sometimes lies fallow for a season.
Outwardly speaks, is spoken to,
works and plays and loves and sleeps
yet is dormant.
There is a cycle, never still.
For both, the seasons move
and there comes to each a spring.

 ELIZABETH SEARLE LAMB
  (1917–2005)

HAPPINESS

I am still determined to be cheerful and happy
in whatever situation I may be, for I have also
learned from experience that the greater part
of our happiness or misery depends on our
dispositions and not on our circumstances.

✎ MARTHA WASHINGTON
(1731–1802)

THE WISDOM TO KNOW

There have been times
when I've allowed insignificant things
to overwhelm my life
and get the better of me.
There have been times
when I have been unforgiving
of myself and others.
When I caused hurt
where I could have healed,
when I had spoken
though silence was best.
Allow me to learn from these things
and let them go.
Allow me the wisdom to know
that at the time
I did my best.

⮌ CORRINE DE WINTER

THE STONE

was heavy.
The family carried it
with them, all day.
Not one
could bear
its weight, alone.
Yet how they loved it.
No other stone had
its denseness,
its particular way
of bending the light.
They could not take
the stone
out in public,
had to keep it home,

let it sing songs

in its own strange language,

syllables of schist and shale.

When the mother's back ached,

the father took the stone

for a while, then passed it

from sister to sister.

The stone

became a part of them,

a bit of granite

in the spine,

a shard of calcite

in the heart.

Sometimes

its weight

pressed them

thin, transparent

as wildflowers

left in the dictionary.

Sometimes

it was

lighter

than air.

The stone

did not talk.

But it shone.

꿍 BARBARA CROOKER

WAITING

All around us we observe a pregnant creation.
The difficult times of pain throughout the world
are simply birth pangs. But it's not only around us;
it's within us. The Spirit of God is arousing us
within. We're also feeling the birth pangs. These
sterile and barren bodies of ours are yearning
for full deliverance. That is why waiting does not
diminish us, any more than waiting diminishes a
pregnant mother. We are enlarged in the waiting.
We, of course, don't see what is enlarging us.
But the longer we wait, the larger we become,
and the more joyful our expectancy.

∾ ROMANS 8:19–25
(THE MESSAGE)

ALL LIFE IS AN EXPERIMENT

All life is an experiment. The more experiments you make the better. What if they are a little coarse, and you may get your coat soiled or torn? What if you do fail, and get fairly rolled in the dirt once or twice?

～ RALPH WALDO EMERSON
(1803–1882)

IF WE ONLY UNDERSTOOD

Could we only draw the curtain
that surrounds each other's lives,
See the naked heart and spirit,
know what spur to action drives.
Often we should find it better,
purer than we judge we should,
We would love each other better,
if we only understood.

∽ AUTHOR UNKNOWN

ACCEPTING THE WORST

When we have accepted the worst, we have nothing
more to lose. And that automatically means—we
have everything to gain.

➯ DALE CARNEGIE
(1888–1955)

HOW DO YOU RECOVER
FROM DISASTER?

Often people have asked me, "How do you recover from disaster?" I don't know any answer except the obvious one: You do it by meeting it and going on. From each you learn something, from each you acquire strength and confidence in yourself to meet the next one when it comes.

⌐ ELEANOR ROOSEVELT
(1884–1962)

IF I HAD MY LIFE TO LIVE OVER

If I had my life to live over again,
I'd dare to make more mistakes next time.
I'd relax.
I would limber up.
I would be sillier than I've been this trip.
I would take fewer things seriously.
I would take more chances.
I would climb more mountains and swim more rivers.
I would eat more ice cream and less beans.
I would perhaps have more actual troubles,
but I'd have fewer imaginary ones.

✒ NADINE STAIR

seven

GRATITUDE

STRANGE BLESSINGS

Life can be puzzling.
Just when everything is going so smoothly,
Out of the blue   in sails a storm—
  in the guise of an illness, accident,
  or disease.

It's natural to ask God,
"Why me?"   "Why now?"
We're told that God works in mysterious ways,
so it's only by taking the time to turn inward
  as our misfortune has forced us to do—
we realize that rather than focusing
on how much we have lost,
our reflection has helped us to see
how much
we still have.

↜ CAROLYN MATTHEWS

THE UNCERTAINTY OF LIFE

Probably the worst,
and the best,
part of life
is its uncertainty . . .

Never knowing
what challenges
and opportunities
just being alive
will give each of us.

↜ JUDITH A. BILLINGS

SONG

A small bird sang
In the dark of night,
Thinking perhaps that dawn
Lay just beyond
The quarter hour.
Why did he sing . . .
If not to me who lay
Tired and tossing
And wide awake?
Perhaps that small bird
Sang again before the dawn.
I heard him not.
I slept, my heart
Eased by his small burst
Of dark night song.

ELIZABETH SEARLE LAMB
(1917–2005)

AFTER THE EPIPHANY

I still rise every morning
and brush my teeth.
Sometimes I complain
if the coffee is cold
or the soup is too hot.
I often wish
I were five pounds thinner
and didn't have lines
tugging at the edge of my lips.
I get tired.
I feel angry.
I worry about my kids.
I want people to call back,
and things to work
the way they should.

I daydream about places
I'd like to go,
and things I ought to have said.

But now,
I linger in the morning
just so I can listen
to wind whispers,
And the joyous cacophony
of bird songs.
I walk with my eyes open
and my head up,
And I watch
the ballet of tree boughs.
I touch the roses.
I smell the dew
upon their velvet lips.

I sit by myself for long hours
and never feel lonely.
I work, calm.
I wait for spirit voices
to soul-talk.
I know that to be alive
is everything.
I rejoice.

~ ELAYNE CLIFT

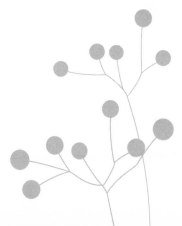

WE ARE BLEST BY EVERYTHING

Excerpt from "Dialogue of Self and Soul"

I am content to follow to its source,
Every event in action or in thought;
Measure the lot; forgive myself the lot!
When such as I cast out remorse

So great a sweetness flows into the breast
We must laugh and we must sing,
We are blest by everything,
Everything we look upon is blest.

⌐ WILLIAM BUTLER YEATS
   (1865–1939)

THE PRESENT

The past plays tag
with the future, and
at the very second
their hands touch,
that is the present,
quicksilver moments
to savor like rare wine.

So celebrate the bitter,
the tart, the sweet
of the here and now,
all before it succumbs
to the pull of what was
and vanishes into a fog
of what might have been.

↶ SUSAN ROGERS NORTON

FERTILE GROUND

What once seemed such a curse has become a blessing. All the agony that threatened to destroy my life now seems like the fertile ground for greater trust, stronger hope, and deeper love.

 HENRI J. M. NOUWEN
(1932–1996)

THE DANCE OF LIFE

Nature blesses us daily:
birds burst into song just as we pass by,
thunderstorms dissolve the dust of drought,
clouds melt away to reveal distant mountains,
stars emerge, glowing against a velvet sky.

Others bless us:
strangers share smiles,
someone gives us a hug,
a colleague defends us at work,
loving friends surround us during a crisis.

Responding to these blessings,
our hearts expand, and we know
we too participate in life's divine dance,
giving and receiving blessings.

↩ SUZANNE C. COLE

GRATITUDE WAITS PATIENTLY

While we cry ourselves to sleep, gratitude waits
patiently to console and reassure us; there is a
landscape larger than the one we can see.

～ SARAH BAN BREATHNACH

eight

INSPIRATION

PROMISE

This day is an open road
stretching out before you.
Roll down the windows.
Step into your life,
as if it were a fast car.
Even in industrial parks,
trees are covered with white blossoms,
festive as brides, and the air is soft
as a well-washed shirt on your arms.
The grass has turned implausibly green.
Tomorrow, the world will begin again,
another fresh start. The blue sky stretches,
shakes out its tent of light. Even dandelions
glitter in the lawn, a handful of golden change.

〜 BARBARA CROOKER

LOOK TO THIS DAY

Look to this day
for it is life
the very life of life.
In its brief course lie all
the realities and truths of existence
the joy of growth
the splendor of action
the glory of power.
For yesterday is but a memory
and tomorrow is only a vision.
But today well lived
makes every yesterday a memory
of happiness
and every tomorrow a vision of hope.
Look well, therefore, to this day!

◝ ANCIENT SANSKRIT POEM

A DOG'S OUTLOOK

Each day comes to your dog new and fresh and full of promise; your dog is not bounded by days of the week, business meetings, deadlines, weekly shopping expeditions, or other obligations and commitments that prevent you from looking forward to the day.

Perhaps it's time to start today to adopt more of your canine's outlook on life. Each morning can be a new beginning—a time for joy and play, a time for fresh air and sunshine, a time for bounding around, a time of canine delight!

⌒ AMY DEAN

CHEROKEE SAYING

Don't let yesterday use up
too much of today.

∽ AUTHOR UNKNOWN

YOUR STRENGTH

The past is gone.
Today is full of possibilities.
With each breath I will be aware of the
strength at hand.

— HAZELDEN FOUNDATION

JUMP!

Whatever it is
That I think I am
I am that, and so much more
How many times do I limit myself
Thinking small
When life is large
Feigning weakness
When I have the strength to move mountains
Bowing low
When I should hold my head high
Coloring inside the lines
Fearing to step outside the box
Where all the wonders of life await
JUMP!

ᵔ NANCY LYNCH GIBSON

I SHALL NOT BE CONTAINED

With one hand stretched and reaching
    as I let go,
palm facing the sky,
with the other hand I gather in:
I shall not be contained
by grief or loss
to a smaller expression.
Into this small room I gather the world
    of all voices,
a confusing melody of delightful
    contradictions;
hard to know who is coming in, who
    is going out—
and my door is like a tree,
leaves dancing, calling to the birds.

I shall not be contained.

What contains me shall be the breath of
    mountains,
and songs that drift in rivers
flowing over rocks rounded to a harmony
by gentle blue fingers.

Nothing shall break the day's length;
When I find jagged rocks in my path
I place them in the river's songs.

 RAMNATH SUBRAMANIAN

A MIRACLE IS COMING

Get ready.
Prepare yourself.
Expect it,
then accept it.
Don't get too busy,
too self-concerned
to miss it.
God loves to do
great things in your life!

— SUSAN ROGERS NORTON

THE THING IS

to love life, to love it even
when you have no stomach for it,
and everything you've held dear
crumbles like burnt paper in your hands,
your throat filled with the silt of it.
When grief sits with you, its tropical heat
thickening the air, heavy as water
more fit for gills than lungs;
when grief weights you like your own flesh
only more of it, an obesity of grief.
you think, *how long can a body withstand this?*
Then you hold life like a face
between your palms, a plain face,
no charming smile, no violet eyes,
and you say, yes, I will take you
I will love you, again.

⇜ ELLEN BASS

THE PRESENCE OF SORROW

The presence of sorrow and hardship in the lives
of others, however, does not mean that all is loss.
Often that which appears to be misfortune can,
with ingenuity and the right mental attitude,
be turned to positive ends.

If our vocabulary did not contain the words trouble,
adversity, calamity, and grief, it could not contain
the words bravery, patience, and self-sacrifice.

Those who know no hardships will know no
hardihood. Those who face no calamity will need
no courage. Mysterious though it is, the human
characteristics we admire most grow in a soil with a
strong mixture of trouble.

> REVEREND DALE E. TURNER
(1917–2006)

BRAVE AND HAPPY LIFE

Happiness comes more from loving than being loved; and often when our affection seems wounded it is only our vanity bleeding. To love, and to be hurt often, and to love again—this is the brave and happy life.

   ~ J. E. BUCHROSE

CONSTELLATIONS

We find our way in the dark
using light from the lives of others.
Their sufferings and celebrations
are like constellations in the midnight sky,
orienting patterns above the horizon.
Tracing their paths through the night,
we connect our stories to one another;
circling together, we turn toward morning.

～ REVEREND J. LYNN JAMES

HOPE RISING

Rising above the cataclysmic flames
a dove,
wings folding into themselves
all opposition,
hope beating strongly despite
soot-singed breast.
As long as she yet flies,
so live we all.

⌁ SUZANNE C. COLE

SPINNING THE COMPASS

Broken compasses of my old broken life
at last, perhaps, are thrown away.

I will invent a new geometry.

But the perfection of a circle lurks
beyond pond ripples or a ring of smoke.

My patterns stay as scattered as the stars.
Galaxies spill over in their dance.
I still must learn what orbits to describe.

But I will learn to chart the sky.

  ~ ELISAVIETTA RITCHIE

BIRTH IS A BEGINNING

Birth is a beginning
And death a destination.
And life is a journey:
From childhood to maturity
And youth to age;
From innocence to awareness
And ignorance to knowing;
And then, perhaps, to wisdom;
From weakness to strength
Or strength to weakness—
And often back again;
From health to sickness
And back, we pray, to health again;
From offense to forgiveness
From loneliness to love,
From joy to gratitude,

From pain to compassion,
And grief to understanding—
From fear to faith;
From defeat to defeat to defeat—
Until, looking backward or ahead,
We see that victory lies
Not at some high place along the way,
But in having made the journey, stage
    by stage,
A sacred pilgrimage.
Birth is a beginning
And death a destination.
And life is a journey,
A sacred pilgrimage—
To life everlasting.

∾ RABBI ALVIN I. FINE

AUTHOR INDEX

PERMISSIONS AND ACKNOWLEDGMENTS

Grateful acknowledgment is made to the authors and publishers for the use of the following material. Every effort has been made to contact original sources. If notified, the publisher will be pleased to rectify an omission in future editions.

Ellen Bass for "The Thing Is." www.ellenbass.com

Berkley Publishing Group for "A Dog's Outlook" from *First Light* by Amy E. Dean, copyright © 1997 by Amy E. Dean. Used by permission of Berkley Publishing Group, a division of Penguin Group (USA) Inc.

Denis Berry for "All Things Pass" by Lao-Tzu, adapted by Dr. Timothy Leary, from *Leary's Psychedelic Prayers,* copyright © 1972, Academy Editions. Reprinted by kind permission of Denis Berry, trustee of Dr. Timothy Leary's trust.

Heather Berry for "Fostering Faith."

Ann Reisfeld Boutté for "It Was Just a Hug."

Pamela Burke for "Cutting Our Hair Before Chemo."

Mirabai Bush for "Pain and Suffering." Reprinted by kind permission of Mirabai Bush. www.mirabaibush.com

Frog Ltd. for "May We Never Give Up Hope" by Andrew Harvey. From *The Way of Passion* by Andrew Harvey, published by Frog Ltd., copyright © 1994 by Andrew Harvey. Reprinted by permission of the publisher.

Nancy Lynch Gibson for "Jump!"

Michael S. Glaser for "Beginning Again." www.michaelsglaser.com

Maryanne Hannan for "Perseverance." www.mhannan.com

Harcourt Inc. for "Don't Wish Me Happiness" by Anne Morrow Lindbergh. Excerpt from *Bring Me a Unicorn: Diaries and Letters of Anne Morrow Lindbergh 1922–1928*, copyright © 1972 by Anne Morrow Lindbergh, reprinted by permission of Harcourt Inc.

HarperCollins Publishers Inc. for "Going to a Special Place" by Macrina Wiederkehr, one paragraph from page 138 from *A Tree Full of Angels* by Macrina Wiederkehr, copyright © 1988 by Macrina Wiederkehr. Reprinted by permission of HarperCollins Publishers Inc.

Sharon Hudnell for "After the Pink Slip," "Believe," "Changes," and "Resilience."

Reverend J. Lynn James for "Constellations." www.lynnjames.net

Elizabeth Searle Lamb for "Song" and "Winter Fields."

Susan Landon for "The Puddle-Jumper," "Tomato Worms," and "Who Would Have Hoped."

Arlene Gay Levine for "Celebration," "Travel," and "Worry Balm." www.arlenegaylevine.com

Judith A. Lindberg for "Memo" and "Twilight."

Maude Meehan for "Coin of This Realm."

Leslie A. Neilson for "Just for Today."

Susan Rogers Norton for "Courage," "A Miracle Is Coming," and "The Present."

Marian Olson for "The Promise" and "When a Marriage Fails."

Elisavietta Ritchie for "Spinning the Compass." www.elisaviettaandclyde.com

Hilda Lachney Sanderson for "Acceptance."

Joanna Catherine Scott for "After the Funeral."

Rabbi Rami M. Shapiro for "Renewal." www.rabbirami.com

Joan Stephen for "Pleasures."

Stone Bridge Press for "Bound Angle" by Leza Lowitz. From *Yoga Poems: Lines to Unfold By*, by Leza Lowitz. Copyright © 2000 by Leza Lowitz. Reprinted by permission of Stone Bridge Press, Berkeley, California.

Ramnath Subramanian for "I Shall Not Be Contained."

ABOUT THE AUTHOR

June Cotner is the author or editor of twenty-nine books, including the best-selling *Graces*, *Bedside Prayers*, and *Dog Blessings*. Altogether her books have sold more than one million copies.

June's latest love and avocation is giving presentations on adopting prisoner-trained shelter dogs. In 2011, she adopted Indy, a chocolate lab/Doberman mix (a LabraDobie!), from the Freedom Tails program at Stafford Creek Corrections Center in Aberdeen, Washington. June works with Indy daily to build on the wonderful obedience skills he mastered in the program. She and Indy have appeared on the television shows *AM Northwest* in Portland, Oregon, and *New Day Northwest* in Seattle.

A graduate of the University of California at Berkeley, June is the mother of two grown children and lives in Poulsbo, Washington, with her husband. Her hobbies include yoga, hiking, and playing with her two grandchildren.

For more information, please visit June's Web site at www.JuneCotner.com.